Grandmas
GONE WILD

RUNNING PRESS
PHILADELPHIA · LONDON

9   8   7   6   5   4   3   2   1
Digit on the right indicates the number of this printing

Library of Congress Control Number: 2006931039

ISBN-10: 0-7624-2976-3
ISBN-13: 978-0-7624-2976-9

Cover and interior designed by Corinda Cook
Photography researched by Susan Oyama
Typography: Caslon, Baskerville, Bellevue, Avenir, Bodega, Claredon, Mod, Monotype Sorts,
Poppl Residenz, Script, and TF Roux

This book may be ordered by mail from the publisher. Please include $2.50 for postage and handling.
But try your bookstore first!

Running Press Book Publishers
2300 Chestnut Street
Philadelphia, PA 19103-4371

Visit us on the web!
www.runningpress.com

Contents

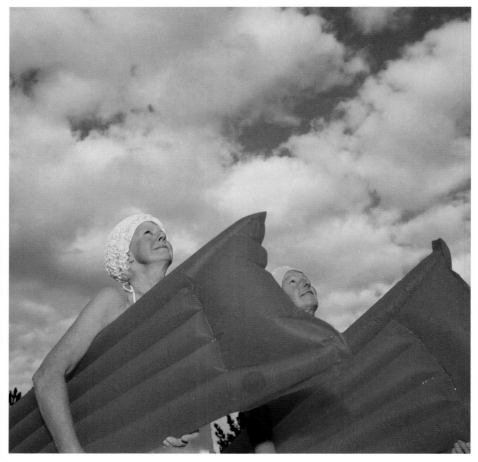

Introduction

Most of us are conditioned to expect certain behavior from grandmothers. We expect a smile of delight and fresh baked cookies when we arrive at their doors, a warm embrace before we leave to drive home or a comforting anecdote when we have a bad day. We have come to accept these cozy images of grandmothers alongside many other beliefs. Grandmas are wise. Grandmas are forgiving. Grandmas are caring. But what about grandmas gone wild?

Grandmas gone wild are our young-hearted conspirators. They wear odd clothing and keep us on our toes with pranks and jokes. These women unabashedly speak their minds to strangers while we pretend not to feel uncomfortable. They wander around the backyard and spy on their neighbors. They are playful, defiant, fun-loving, and hysterical sources of joy. For grandmas gone wild, youth is simply a state of mind.

Gathered here are words on aging, fun, strength, family, and remembering from well-known people who have used age-old insights to describe the behavior of these beloved members of society. Their thought-provoking sentiments seem oddly appropriate here. The photographs prove that traditional thoughts about grandmothers can sometimes ring true in unexpected ways when grandmas go wild!

On Aging

My grandson was visiting one day when he asked,
"Gramma, do you know how you and God are alike?"
I mentally polished my halo while I asked,
"No, how are we alike?"
"You're both old," he replied.

Author Unknown

Those of us who
are old can afford to
live dangerously.
We have less to lose.

Maggie Kuhn (1905–1990)

Civic Activist

A passionate interest in what you do is the secret of enjoying life, perhaps the secret of a long life, whether it is helping old people or children or making cheese or growing earthworms.

Julia Child (1912–2004)

Chef and Author

Beauty is accepting what you are, who you are, and how old you are. Ugliness is when you try to be something else.

Sophia Loren, b. 1934

Actor

I LOOK FORWARD TO GROWING OLD AND WISE AND AUDACIOUS.

Glenda Jackson, b. 1937

Actor

I don't want to *fight* old age, but I'm not about to invite it to live in, either. I want a nice symbiotic relationship with it, where we are totally unaware of each other.

Betty White, b. 1924

Actor

If you pretend old age is not going to happen, it will fall right on you.

Julia Child (1912–2004)

Chef and Author

Perhaps one has to be very old before one learns to be amused rather than shocked.

Pearl S. Buck (1892–1973)

Author

Judging by the world's press

I am the only grandmother in the world.

Marlene Dietrich (1901–1992)

Actor

If you don't have wrinkles, you haven't laughed enough.

Phyllis Diller, b. 1917

Comedian

What is it about a grandparent
that is so lovely?
I'd like to say that grandparents are
God's gifts to children.
And if they can but see, hear,
and feel what these people have to give,
they can mature at a fast rate.

Bill Cosby, b. 1937

Comedian

Grandchildren don't make a man feel old; it's the knowledge that he's married to a grandmother.

G. Norman Collie (1859–1942)

Scientist

On Fun

Time and trouble will tame an advanced
young woman,
but an advanced old woman is uncontrollable
by any earthly force.

Dorothy Sayers (1893–1957)

Author

*Well! Some people talk
of morality,
and some of religion,
but give me a
little snug property.*

Maria Edgeworth (1767–1849)

Author

Life is a big thing, it's got size, and you shouldn't be applying your passion to puny things. Life is a struggle for the human heart and the human spirit, a struggle between good and bad for good and bad.

Peggy Noonan, b. 1950
Author

When grandparents enter the door, discipline flies out the window.

Ogden Nash (1902–1971)

Poet

Grandmother,
family-proud
and so of house,
with hob black-
leaded, glistening
like a raven's wings
and brass like
gold untarnished.

Brian Harris, b. 1933

Poet

Grandmas . . . can shed the yoke of responsibility, relax, and enjoy their grandchildren in a way that was not possible when they were raising their own children. And they can glow in the realization that here is their seed of life that will harvest generations to come.

Erma Bombeck (1927–1996)
Author

On
Strength

Nothing can help us face the unknown future
with more courage and optimism
than remembering the glory moments,
and everybody has a few of them.

Eda LeShan (1922–2002)

Author

There is a fountain of youth: it is your mind, your talents, the creativity you bring to your life and the lives of the people you love. When you learn to tap this source, you will have truly defeated age.

Sophia Loren, b. 1934

Actor

My grandmother was a very tough woman. She buried three husbands and two of them were just napping.

Rita Rudner, b. 1956

Actor, Comedian, and Author

You have to stay in shape. My grandmother, she started walking five miles a day when she was 60. She's 97 today and we don't know where the hell she is.

Ellen DeGeneres, b. 1958
Comedian

She was a buxom grandmother noted for her detective stories, who gazed mournfully at the camera as if deploring either the bloodiness of her craft or the size of her advance.

P. D. James, b. 1920
Author

MY GRANDMOTHER IS OVER EIGHTY
AND STILL DOESN'T NEED GLASSES.
DRINKS RIGHT OUT OF THE BOTTLE.

Henny Youngman (1906–1998)
Comedian

In the effort to give good and
comforting answers to the young
questioners whom we love,
we very often arrive at good and
comforting answers for ourselves.

Ruth Goode (1905–1997)

Author

The purpose of living is to get old enough to have something to say. . . .

M.F.K. Fisher (1908–1992)
Author

On Family

If a tie is like kissing your sister,
losing is like kissing you grandmother with her teeth out.

George Brett, b. 1953
Baseball Player

A house needs a grandma in it.

Louisa May Alcott (1832–1888)

Author

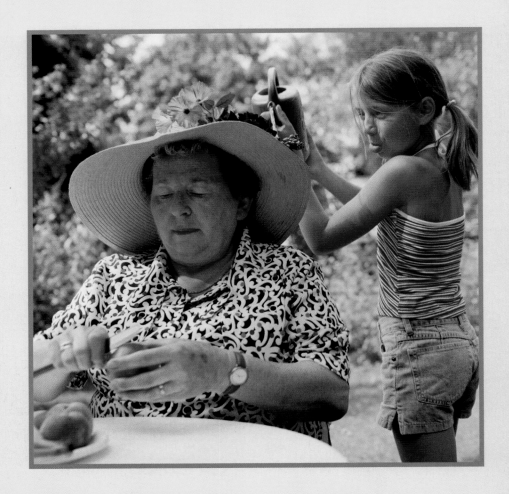

Have children while your parents are still young enough to take care of them.

Rita Rudner, b. 1956
Actor, Comedian, and Author

Nothing is more important to human happiness than to be part of a fractious, forgiving, warm, tightly knit family.

Marjorie Holmes (1910–2002)

Author

A grandmother corrects your grammar and wipes imaginary dirt from our cheeks.

Sara Spurrier (age 12)

*Having grandchildren is
the best of all possible worlds.
I don't have any
responsibility for them—
I just do all the fun stuff.*

Author Unknown

Grandchildren provide us with some of our proudest occasions, some of our tenderest experiences, and, without question, some of our funniest moments.

Catharine Brandt (1905–1997)

Author

Grandma always made you feel she had been waiting to see just you all day and now the day was complete.

Marcy DeMaree
Author

Grandmother-grandchild relationships are simple.
Grandmas are short on criticism and long on love.

Author Unknown

Grandmothers don't have to do anything except be there . . . It is enough if they drive us to the market, where the pretend horse is, and have lots of dimes ready. Or if they take us for walks, they slow down past things like pretty leaves or caterpillars. They should never "hurry up."

Patsy Gray (age 9)

There are only two families in the world, my old grandmother used to say, the Haves and the Have-nots.

Miguel de Cervantes (1547–1616)

Author

On Remembering

Do the young seek absolute truth?
Take me along, too.
After all, I might have earlier crossed this way,
and when you feel as quicksand,
I might feel as concrete, the path hardened by values
I learned when I passed before.

Pearl Bailey (1918–1990)

Actor and Author

That was one of the good things
about getting old: you weren't
perpetually in a hurry . . .
There was time to stop and look,
and, looking, to remember.

Rosamunde Pilcher, b. 1924
Author

Things are new even at the age when we are supposed to have seen everything.

Louise Erdrich, b. 1954

Author

I've had lots of kids come up

and ask for my autograph.

I've had a grandmother stop

me and ask me if I know

a good place to buy underwear.

Prince William, b. 1982
The Prince of Wales

Growing older frees you from all sorts of previous restrictions and guilt.

Betty Friedan (1921–2006)

Political Activist

A grandmother pretends she doesn't know who you are on Halloween.

Erma Bombeck (1927–1996)

Author

*Holding these babies
in my arms makes me realize
the miracle my
husband and I began.*

Betty Ford, b. 1918

Former First Lady

Photography Credits